# THE 10X REVOLUTION

## THE ROADMAP TO UNSTOPPABLE SUCCESS

### By Kebison Ibra

The 10x revolution is a powerful concept that has been embraced by many successful individuals and organizations. It states that by thinking and acting in a way that is 10 times bigger, bolder, and more audacious than what seems reasonable or attainable, one can unlock the full potential of their ideas and unleash exponential growth. Whether you're an entrepreneur looking to launch a new business, a creative seeking to make an impact, or simply someone looking to make a change in their life, the 10x revolution provides a roadmap to help you break free from mediocrity and achieve greatness.

10x revolution is the idea that adopting a 10X mindset and approach can bring about a profound transformation in your life and career. The 10X approach involves setting ambitious, yet achievable, goals and pursuing them with unrelenting focus and determination. By embracing this mindset, individuals can break through their limitations and achieve levels of success they never thought possible. The 10X revolution is about recognizing the power of your own potential and taking control of your life and career through intentional and strategic action. It's about making a conscious decision to think big, act boldly, and pursue your dreams with relentless determination. In essence, it's about creating a personal revolution that propels you toward the life and career of your dreams.

# CHAPTER ONE
## SET MASSIVE AND AUDACIOUS GOALS

Set massive, audacious goals that are 10 times greater than what you believe you can achieve. Individuals should set massive, audacious goals that are 10 times greater than what they believe they can achieve. The goal of this principle is to challenge individuals to think beyond their limitations and to set goals that are truly transformational. The 10x revolution is designed to help individuals overcome complacency and mediocrity, and to push themselves to new heights.

The concept of setting 10X goals is based on the idea that people often limit themselves by what they believe is possible. By setting big, bold goals, individuals can create a sense of urgency and intensity in their approach to achieving these goals. When individuals have a sense of urgency and intensity, they are more likely to take bold and decisive action, which can result in significant progress towards their goals.

In addition to creating a sense of urgency and intensity, setting 10X goals can also help individuals focus their energy and attention on what is truly important. When individuals have big, bold goals, they are less likely to get bogged down by small, incremental improvements and are more likely to stay focused on what is truly important. This type of goal setting can also help individuals maintain a long-term perspective and keep their eye on the prize, even when they encounter obstacles or setbacks.

It's important to note that setting 10X goals does not mean setting unrealistic or unachievable goals. The 10x revolution is not about setting impossible goals, but rather about pushing the limits of what is considered possible. When setting 10X goals, individuals should be realistic and ensure that their goals are achievable, but also challenging.

When setting 10X goals, individuals should be clear and specific about what they want to achieve. They should also establish a timeline for achieving their goals and create a plan of action for how they will achieve them. This plan should include specific and measurable steps that they can take to move closer to their goals.

In conclusion, it is about setting big, bold, and audacious goals that are 10 times greater than what individuals believe they can achieve. The idea is to challenge individuals to think beyond what is considered possible, to create a sense of urgency and intensity in their approach to achieving their goals, and to focus on what is truly important. By setting 10X goals, individuals can overcome complacency and mediocrity, push themselves to new heights, and achieve truly transformational results. clerical examples; Set massive, audacious goals that are 10 times greater than what they believe they can achieve. This principle can be applied in a clerical setting, where individuals can use it to challenge themselves to think beyond their current limitations and to set big, bold goals that can transform their careers.

One way that clerks can apply the 10X Productivity is by setting ambitious goals for their productivity. For example, if a clerk typically completes 10 tasks in a day, they can set a goal to complete 100 tasks in a day. This type of goal is 10 times greater than what the clerk believes is possible and will challenge them to push their limits and increase their productivity. The sense of urgency and intensity that is created by setting such a goal can help the clerk focus their energy and attention on what is truly important and can result in significant progress towards their goal.

Another way that clerks can apply the 10X Productivity is by setting ambitious goals for their professional development. For example, if a clerk is typically responsible for filing and organizing documents, they can set a goal to become a department manager within the next 5 years. This type of goal is 10 times greater than what the clerk believes is possible and will challenge them to think beyond their current role and to take bold and decisive action to achieve their goal. By setting this goal, the clerk can focus on acquiring the skills and knowledge necessary to become a department manager, and can work towards achieving this goal with a sense of urgency and intensity.

It's important to note that when clerks set 10X goals, they should be realistic and ensure that their goals are achievable, but also challenging. Clerks should also establish a timeline for achieving their goals and create a plan of action for how they will achieve them. This plan should include specific and measurable steps that they can take to move closer to their goals, such as taking relevant courses or networking with department managers.

Setting Massive goal can be applied in a clerical setting to help clerks challenge themselves to think beyond their current limitations and to set big, bold goals that can transform their careers. By setting 10X goals for productivity and professional development, clerks can overcome complacency and mediocrity, push themselves to new heights, and achieve truly transformational results.

# CHAPTER TWO
## START WITH MASSIVE ACTION

This is a crucial principle for success and personal growth. The idea is that success and growth are not achieved through incremental, gradual steps, but rather through bold, decisive actions that create momentum and push you towards your goals.

The concept of massive action is rooted in the belief that our thoughts, beliefs, and actions are all interconnected, and that success is largely a result of taking consistent and sustained action towards your goals. In order to achieve success, you must be willing to take bold and decisive steps, and to continuously push yourself out of your comfort zone.

One of the key benefits of massive action is that it creates momentum and drives results. By taking large, decisive actions, you can quickly move closer to your goals and start seeing real progress. This momentum can be especially powerful when it comes to overcoming obstacles and obstacles, as taking massive action can help you overcome resistance and push through challenges.

Another benefit of massive action is that it helps you develop a strong sense of confidence and self-belief. When you take bold and decisive actions towards your goals, you demonstrate to yourself and others that you are capable and committed which can boost your self-esteem and give you the motivation you need to keep pushing forward.

However, taking massive action is not always easy. It often requires taking risks, pushing yourself out of your comfort zone, and facing challenges head-on. This can be scary and intimidating, especially if you are used to taking small, incremental steps. But, by embracing this fear and taking massive action anyway, you can demonstrate to yourself that you are capable of more than you thought, and you can build a foundation of confidence and resilience that will help you in all areas of your life.

To get the most out of the 10x revolution, it's important to be intentional and purposeful in your actions. This means setting clear and specific goals, developing a plan for how you will achieve these goals, and taking consistent, deliberate steps towards your goals every day. It's also important to surround yourself with the right people, as the support and encouragement of others can be instrumental in helping you achieve your goals.

Finally, it's important to keep in mind that taking massive action is a lifelong commitment. Success is not achieved overnight, and it requires ongoing effort, dedication, and perseverance. But, by starting with massive action and consistently taking bold, decisive steps towards your goals, you can achieve more than you thought was possible and live the life you've always dreamed of.

Taking massive action is a powerful principle that can help you achieve success and personal growth. By taking bold and decisive actions towards your goals, you can create momentum, build confidence, and overcome obstacles to achieve more than you thought was possible. Whether you're looking to advance your career, improve your relationships, or achieve your personal goals, starting with massive action is a key step in the right direction.

To help clarify this principle, here are some examples of massive action in a clerical setting:

Filing all overdue documents within a day, instead of dragging it out for a week.

Offering to take on additional responsibilities at work, even if it means working longer hours or taking on tasks outside your job description.

Volunteering to lead a new project or take charge of a difficult task, even if you have never done it before.

Implementing a new, more efficient system for organizing and storing important company information.

Setting daily, weekly, and monthly goals, and taking concrete steps to achieve them, no matter how small.

One way to take massive action in a clerical setting is by taking on additional responsibilities at work. This might mean volunteering for tasks outside of your job description, or offering to take on additional projects when others are overwhelmed. For example, if you work in a busy office and your colleagues are struggling to keep up with a large workload, you could offer to help with some of their tasks. This would demonstrate your willingness to help and your dedication to the company, which could lead to future opportunities and advancement within the organization.

Another way to take massive action in a clerical setting is by implementing new, more efficient systems and processes. For example, if you work in an office where there is a lot of paperwork and files, you could suggest implementing a new, more efficient system for organizing and storing these documents. This might involve digitizing paper files, creating a new filing system, or automating certain tasks. By taking the initiative to implement these changes, you can demonstrate your problem-solving skills and your commitment to improving the office's overall efficiency.

A third way to take massive action in a clerical setting is by continuously learning and growing. This might involve enrolling in courses, attending workshops, or seeking out professional development opportunities. For example, if you work in a field that requires a lot of typing and data entry, you could enroll in a course to improve your typing speed and accuracy. This would demonstrate your commitment to continuously improving your skills, and could lead to increased job satisfaction and advancement within your company.

Finally, taking massive action in a clerical setting could also involve setting clear and specific goals for yourself and your work. For example, you might set a goal to improve your typing speed by 10% in the next three months, or to complete a certain number of projects within a specific timeframe. By setting these goals, you can ensure that you are taking deliberate steps towards your professional development and advancement.

Starting with massive action is an important principle for success in a clerical setting. Whether it involves taking on additional responsibilities, implementing new systems and processes, continuously learning and growing, or setting clear and specific goals, taking bold and decisive actions can help you achieve your professional goals and advance your career. By embracing this principle, you can demonstrate your commitment to your work, your problem-solving skills, and your ability to continuously improve and grow.

One person who embodies this concept is Elon Musk, the CEO of SpaceX, Tesla, Neuralink, and The Boring Company. Throughout his career, Musk has demonstrated a remarkable ability to set massive goals and then take the massive action required to achieve them.

Musk was born in South Africa in 1971, and from a young age, he demonstrated a remarkable aptitude for science and technology. He taught himself computer programming at the age of 12 and sold his first computer game at the age of 14. Despite his early success, Musk was not content to simply sit back and enjoy his accomplishments. He was driven to achieve more and to make a difference in the world.

Musk set a massive goal for himself: to help humanity become a multi-planetary species. He believed that by colonizing other planets, humans would be able to ensure their survival and to secure the future of life on Earth. This was a massive goal, but Musk was determined to make it a reality. He founded SpaceX in 2002 with the goal of reducing the cost of space access and to make space exploration more accessible to the general public.

SpaceX has since become one of the leading private space exploration companies in the world. The company has developed reusable rockets and spacecraft, which have dramatically reduced the cost of space access. In 2012, SpaceX became the first privately funded company to send a spacecraft to the International Space Station. The company has since sent numerous missions to the ISS and has even sent astronauts to the station on its Dragon spacecraft.

In addition to his work at SpaceX, Musk has also set massive goals for himself in the fields of electric vehicles and sustainable energy. He founded Tesla in 2003 with the goal of producing electric vehicles that were not only environmentally friendly but also fun to drive. Despite widespread skepticism, Musk was able to achieve this goal, and Tesla has since become one of the leading electric vehicle manufacturers in the world.

Musk has also set his sights on sustainable energy and has founded companies such as SolarCity and The Boring Company to help achieve this goal. SolarCity provides solar panels and energy storage systems to homes and businesses, while The Boring Company aims to reduce traffic congestion in cities by digging tunnels for high-speed transportation systems.

Elon Musk is a remarkable example of the power of setting massive goals and taking massive action to achieve them. Throughout his career, Musk has demonstrated a remarkable ability to set big, audacious goals, and then take the massive action required to make them a reality. His work at SpaceX, Tesla, Neuralink, and The Boring Company has had a profound impact on the world, and he continues to push the boundaries of what is possible. The story of Elon Musk demonstrates that with hard work, determination, and a willingness to take bold and decisive action, anyone can achieve their biggest and most audacious goals, and make a meaningful and lasting impact on the world.

Another person who embodies this concept is Muhammad Ali, widely regarded as one of the greatest boxers of all time. Throughout his career, Ali set massive goals for himself and took the massive action required to achieve them.

Muhammad Ali was born Cassius Marcellus Clay Jr. in Louisville, Kentucky, in 1942. From a young age, Ali was drawn to boxing, and he began training at the age of 12. Despite his natural talent, Ali faced many challenges in his early career. He was often underestimated and overlooked, and he was told that he would never become a champion.

However, Ali refused to be discouraged by these setbacks. He set a massive goal for himself: to become the heavyweight champion of the world. He knew that this was a tall order, but he was determined to make it a reality. He trained tirelessly, honing his skills and perfecting his technique. He also developed a powerful mental game, focusing on visualization and positive self-talk.

In 1964, Ali achieved his goal when he defeated Sonny Liston to become the heavyweight champion of the world. He was just 22 years old at the time, and he was the youngest boxer to win the heavyweight title. Ali's victory was a massive upset, and it stunned the boxing world.

However, Ali did not stop there. He continued to set massive goals for himself, and he continued to take massive action to achieve them. Throughout his career, Ali faced many challenges, including political and social obstacles, but he never wavered in his determination to achieve his goals.

In 1967, Ali refused to be drafted into the Vietnam War on religious and political grounds, citing his opposition to the war and his status as a conscientious objector. He was stripped of his heavyweight title and banned from boxing for several years, but he refused to be discouraged. Instead, he used this time to focus on his activism and to speak out against the war and for social justice.

In 1971, Ali returned to the ring, and he continued to set massive goals for himself. He won several high-profile fights, including the "Fight of the Century" against Joe Frazier and the "Thrilla in Manila" against Frazier. He continued to be a dominant force in the heavyweight division, and he retired in 1981 with a record of 56 wins, 5 losses, and 37 knockouts.

Muhammad Ali, a remarkable example of the power of setting massive goals and taking massive action to achieve them. Throughout his career, Ali demonstrated a remarkable ability to set big, audacious goals, and then take the massive action required to make them a reality. His work as a boxer and as an activist has had a profound impact on the world, and he continues to inspire people to this day. The story of Muhammad Ali demonstrates that with hard work, determination, and a willingness to take bold and decisive action, anyone can achieve their biggest and most audacious goals, and make a meaningful and lasting impact on the world.

# CHAPTER THREE

## MENTAL TOUGHNESS

The concept of Mental toughness is a key aspect of this principle because it requires an individual to have a strong and unyielding mindset in order to successfully achieve these massive goals. It is the ability to stay focused, remain disciplined, and persist in the face of adversity and challenges, even when it seems as though success is unlikely. It requires an individual to push beyond their perceived limits and overcome any obstacles that stand in their way.

Mental toughness is often developed through a combination of nature and nurture. Some people may have a natural tendency towards resilience, while others may have developed this skill through their experiences and environment. However, regardless of one's starting point, mental toughness is a skill that can be developed and strengthened over time with consistent effort and determination.

One of the key components of mental toughness is having a growth mindset, rather than a fixed mindset. A growth mindset is one that is characterized by a belief that one's abilities and intelligence can be developed through effort, while a fixed mindset is one that views abilities and intelligence as inherent and unchanging. Individuals with a growth mindset are more likely to embrace challenges and see them as opportunities for growth and development, rather than as threats to their abilities.

Another key component of mental toughness is having a strong sense of purpose. This means having a clear and compelling reason for why one is pursuing their goals and what they hope to achieve. A strong sense of purpose can provide motivation and drive, even when challenges arise and obstacles seem insurmountable. It also helps to anchor an individual and keep them focused on their goals, even when distractions and temptations arise.

In addition to having a growth mindset and a strong sense of purpose, mental toughness also requires an individual to have a deep commitment to their goals. This means being willing to make sacrifices, take risks, and put in the time and effort required to achieve their goals. It also requires having a strong sense of self-discipline and being able to resist distractions and temptations that can detract from one's efforts.

Mental toughness is also closely linked to one's mindset and beliefs about failure. Individuals who view failure as a necessary part of the learning process, and who are willing to take calculated risks, are more likely to develop mental toughness. On the other hand, individuals who view failure as a reflection of their abilities and who are afraid of taking risks are less likely to develop mental toughness.

Mental toughness is a critical component of the 10x revolution, and is essential for anyone who wants to achieve massive success and push beyond their perceived limits. It requires a combination of a growth mindset, a strong sense of purpose, a deep commitment to one's goals, and a willingness to embrace failure as a necessary part of the learning process. With consistent effort and determination, anyone can develop this skill and achieve their most audacious goals.

One example of mental toughness is the ability to handle stress and pressure. In order to achieve the level of success outlined in the 10x revolution, it is often necessary to take on challenging tasks and meet tight deadlines. Mentally tough individuals are able to handle stress and pressure in a productive and positive way, without letting it interfere with their ability to focus and perform. They are able to maintain a clear and focused mind, even in high-pressure situations, which allows them to make better decisions and achieve their goals.

Another example of mental toughness is the ability to handle setbacks and failures. In order to achieve the level of success outlined in the 10x revolution, it is important to persevere and continue working towards your goals, even when faced with setbacks and failures. Mentally tough individuals are able to bounce back quickly from setbacks and use them as opportunities to learn and grow. They do not let setbacks and failures define them, and they remain motivated and determined to achieve their goals, even in the face of adversity.

A third example of mental toughness is the ability to maintain focus and motivation. In order to achieve the level of success outlined in the 10x revolution, it is important to remain focused on your goals and motivated to work towards them, even in the face of distractions and obstacles. Mentally tough individuals are able to remain focused and motivated, even in the face of challenges, and they are able to prioritize their tasks effectively, which helps them to remain productive and efficient.

A fourth example of mental toughness is the ability to handle criticism and negative feedback. In order to achieve the level of success outlined in the 10x revolution, it is important to be open to feedback and criticism, and to use it as an opportunity to improve and grow. Mentally tough individuals are able to handle criticism and negative feedback in a productive and positive way, without letting it interfere with their ability to focus and perform. They are able to maintain a positive attitude and use criticism and negative feedback as an opportunity to learn and grow.

In order to develop mental toughness, it is important to cultivate a positive and growth-oriented mindset. Mentally tough individuals are able to maintain a positive outlook, even in the face of adversity, and they are able to see challenges and setbacks as opportunities to learn and grow. They are also able to maintain a growth-oriented mindset, which allows them to continuously improve and achieve their goals.

Another key aspect of developing mental toughness is setting achievable and realistic goals. Mentally tough individuals are able to set goals that are realistic and achievable, and they are able to work towards them consistently and with determination. By setting achievable and realistic goals, mentally tough individuals are able to maintain focus and motivation, and they are able to make steady progress towards their goals.

In conclusion, mental toughness is a crucial aspect of the 10x revolution, and it refers to the ability to persevere in the face of adversity, handle stress and pressure, and maintain focus and motivation. In order to develop mental toughness, it is important to cultivate a positive and growth-oriented mindset, set achievable and realistic goals, and be open to feedback and criticism. By developing mental toughness, individuals are able to achieve the level of success outlined in the 10x revolution, and they are able to overcome challenges and obstacles in order to achieve their goals. Lets look at the life of Richard Williams Richard Williams was a man who believed in the power of the 10x revolution, and he used this philosophy to help his daughters,

Venus and Serena, achieve great success in the world of tennis. As the coach and mentor of two of the greatest tennis players of all time, he had a unique understanding of what it took to develop mental toughness and a winning mindset.

The 10x revolution, which was popularized by entrepreneur and motivational speaker Grant Cardone, is based on the idea that one should set their goals 10 times higher than they think they can achieve. This is meant to push individuals beyond their comfort zones and help them to achieve more than they ever thought possible.

Richard believed that this approach was particularly relevant in the world of tennis, where success often comes down to a player's mental toughness and ability to perform under pressure. He encouraged Venus and Serena to embrace the 10x revolution in their own lives and to set their sights on winning the biggest tournaments in the world, rather than just focusing on the next match.

Richard's approach to the 10x revolution was rooted in his own experiences as a self-taught tennis coach. Despite having no prior experience in the sport, he was determined to turn his daughters into champions, and he was willing to do whatever it took to make that happen.

He spent countless hours researching the game and learning from books, videos, and other sources. He also hired top coaches to work with Venus and Serena, and he pushed them to work hard and improve their skills every day.

Despite facing numerous obstacles and setbacks along the way, Richard never lost sight of his vision, and he encouraged his daughters to do the same. He taught them that the key to success was to remain focused on their long-term goals and to never give up, no matter how difficult the journey might be.

Venus and Serena embraced their father's philosophy, and they developed a winning mindset that was centered around mental toughness and the 10x revolution. They set their sights on winning Grand Slam titles and becoming the best players in the world, and they worked tirelessly to achieve their goals.

Over time, their determination and mental toughness paid off, as they went on to become two of the greatest tennis players of all time, with numerous Grand Slam titles and countless victories to their name. They credit much of their success to the lessons they learned from their father about mental toughness and the power of goal-setting.

For Richard, the 10x revolution was more than just a philosophy, it was a way of life. He believed that anyone could achieve greatness if they set their sights high and pushed themselves to their limits. He was a true inspiration to his daughters and to countless others who have been touched by his story.

The lessons that Richard taught his daughters about mental toughness and the 10x revolution are just as relevant today as they were when he first introduced them. In a world where success often comes down to a person's ability to perform under pressure, these principles are more important than ever.

Whether you are a young tennis player, a business person, or simply someone who wants to achieve greatness, the 10x revolution and the lessons of Richard Williams can help you to develop the mental toughness and winning mindset that you need to succeed.

So if you are looking to achieve great things in life, embrace the 10x revolution, set your sights high, and never give up. With hard work, determination, and mental toughness, you can achieve anything that you set your mind to. Just like Venus and Serena Williams, you too can become a champion.

Another prime example of this is the Indian Boxer, Mary Kom, who embodies the spirit of the 10x revolution. Mary Kom, also known as Magnificent Mary, is a five-time world amateur boxing champion and Olympic bronze medallist. She is the only female boxer to have won a medal in each of the seven world championships.

Mary Kom was born in a small village in the Indian state of Manipur. Her parents were farmers, and she grew up in poverty. Despite these challenges, Mary was a determined child who had a passion for boxing. She started boxing at the age of 18 and quickly rose through the ranks to become one of the best boxers in the world.

However, success did not come easily to Mary. She faced many obstacles and challenges along the way. One of the biggest challenges she faced was the lack of support and recognition for women's boxing in India. Women's boxing was not considered a sport in India, and there was very little support or resources available to female boxers.

Despite these challenges, Mary continued to pursue her passion for boxing with determination and resilience. She took massive, bold actions to achieve her goals. For example, she would train for hours every day, often in harsh conditions and with limited resources. She would also travel long distances to attend training sessions and competitions, often at her own expense.

Mary's dedication and hard work paid off, and she soon became one of the best female boxers in the world. She won her first world championship in 2002, and since then, she has won five world championships and an Olympic bronze medal.

Mary's success is a testament to the power of the 10x revolution. By taking massive, bold actions, she was able to overcome the obstacles and challenges that stood in her way. She refused to be held back by societal expectations or lack of resources and continued to push herself to be the best she could be.

In conclusion, Mary Kom's story is a powerful example of how the 10x revolution can help you achieve success. Her determination and resilience in the face of adversity show that success is not just about taking small, incremental steps but about taking massive, bold actions that push you beyond your comfort zone and toward your goals. By embracing the 10x revolution, you can achieve great success, just like Mary Kom.

# CHAPTER FOUR

## BELIEVE IN YOURSELF

This is a crucial aspect of the concept and is closely related to the first three points. The idea behind the 10x revolution is that setting bigger and bolder goals leads to increased motivation, focus, and effort, resulting in higher levels of achievement.

Believing in oneself is a crucial aspect of the 10x revolution because it is the foundation upon which all other elements of the concept are built. Without belief in oneself and one's abilities, it becomes difficult to set challenging goals and take action to achieve them. When an individual lacks self-confidence and self-belief, they are less likely to set ambitious goals, and when faced with obstacles, they are more likely to give up.

Believing in oneself is not just about having a positive attitude, but also about having a deep understanding of one's abilities, strengths, and weaknesses. When an individual believes in themselves, they are more likely to take calculated risks, and they are more likely to trust their instincts and decisions. They are also more likely to seek out new opportunities and take advantage of them, as they are not held back by fear or self-doubt.

Moreover, self-belief also provides an individual with the resilience and persistence needed to overcome obstacles and setbacks. When faced with challenges, those who believe in themselves are more likely to remain focused on their goals, to take action to overcome the obstacles, and to persist in their efforts even when the going gets tough. They are less likely to give up when faced with adversity and are more likely to persevere in their pursuit of success.

To develop and strengthen self-belief, it is important to focus on personal development and growth. This involves taking an honest look at oneself, identifying areas for improvement, and actively working on developing one's skills and abilities. It is also important to seek out feedback from others and to seek out opportunities for growth and development. By doing so, individuals can gain a deeper understanding of their strengths and weaknesses, and they can develop the skills and abilities needed to achieve their goals.

Another important aspect of developing self-belief is to focus on positive self-talk and to surround oneself with positive, supportive individuals. Positive self-talk helps individuals to overcome self-doubt and to remain focused on their goals, even when faced with adversity. Surrounding oneself with positive, supportive individuals helps to build self-confidence, as individuals receive encouragement, support, and motivation from others.

In conclusion, "Believe in yourself," is a crucial aspect of the concept. Without belief in oneself and one's abilities, it becomes difficult to set challenging goals and take action to achieve them. To develop and strengthen self-belief, individuals must focus on personal development and growth, seek out feedback, focus on positive self-talk, and surround themselves with positive, supportive individuals. By doing so, individuals can gain a deeper understanding of their strengths and weaknesses, build self-confidence, and achieve their goals with greater ease and success.

In order to understand the importance of this component, let's take a look at a few examples of how believing in oneself can lead to success.

Example 1: In Starting a Business;

Imagine that you have always had a passion for starting your own business. However, you are plagued by self-doubt and the fear of failure. You do not believe in your abilities to start and run a successful business. As a result, you never take action towards your goal of starting a business.

Now, imagine that instead of letting self-doubt hold you back, you decide to adopt a 10X mindset and believe in yourself. You take action towards your goal and start your own business. Despite the challenges and obstacles that arise, you persist in pursuing your goal and remain optimistic and confident in your abilities.

As a result of your self-belief, you are able to overcome the challenges and obstacles that arise, and your business becomes a success. Your self-belief has given you the confidence to take risks, make bold decisions, and pursue your goals.

Example 2: In Pursuing a Career in Arts;

Let's say that you have always had a passion for painting but have never pursued it as a career because you do not believe in your abilities. You are afraid of failing and do not believe that you have what it takes to be a successful artist.

However, if you adopt a 10X mindset and believe in yourself, you will have the confidence to pursue your passion for painting. You will take action towards your goal, even in the face of obstacles and setbacks. You will persist in pursuing your goal and will remain optimistic and confident in your abilities.

As a result of your self-belief, you will develop your skills and become a successful artist. Your self-belief will give you the confidence to take risks and pursue your goals, even in the face of challenges and obstacles.

Example 3: In improving Athletic Performance;

Imagine that you are an athlete and want to improve your performance. However, you do not believe in your abilities and are afraid of failing. As a result, you do not push yourself to the limits and do not achieve your full potential.

Now, imagine that instead of letting self-doubt hold you back, you adopt a 10X mindset and believe in yourself. You set a goal to improve your performance by 10 times and take action towards that goal. You persist in pursuing your goal, even in the face of challenges and setbacks, and remain optimistic and confident in your abilities.

As a result of your self-belief, you push yourself to the limits and achieve your full potential. Your self-belief gives you the confidence to take risks and pursue your goals, even in the face of challenges and obstacles.

These examples demonstrate the power of self-belief and the importance of the "Believe in Yourself" component of the 10x revolution. When you believe in yourself and your abilities, you are more confident, optimistic, and motivated to pursue your goals. This self-belief will give you the confidence to take risks and overcome obstacles, and will lead to greater success and achievement.

In order to develop self-belief, it is important to focus on your strengths and accomplishments, surround yourself with positive and supportive people, set achievable goals, take action, and be persistent in pursuing your goals. By developing self-belief, you will be able to achieve your full potential and achieve success in all areas of your life.

Before diving to chapter Five, If you are enjoying this video. please Click on the Subscribe Button below, as this will serve as an indicator that I am building an audience that are ready to 10x their thinking, their actions and their life.

.

# CHAPTER FIVE
## Embrace Failure

When you set a 10X goal, you are setting a goal that is significantly larger than what you believe you can achieve. By doing so, you are stepping outside of your comfort zone and putting yourself in a position to potentially fail. However, it is important to remember that failure is not a setback, but rather an opportunity to learn and grow.

One of the benefits of embracing failure is that it allows you to learn from your mistakes. When you fail, you have the opportunity to reflect on what went wrong and identify areas for improvement. This can lead to greater insight and understanding, which can ultimately help you achieve your goals. For example, if you set a goal to double your sales, but fall short, you can use the experience to learn what went wrong and make changes to your approach for the next time.

Embracing failure also helps to build resilience and determination. When you are faced with failure, it can be tempting to give up, but if you choose to keep pushing forward and not let failure define you, you will develop a greater sense of determination and resilience. This will help you to overcome challenges and continue moving forward, even when faced with setbacks.

In addition, embracing failure can also lead to increased creativity and innovation. When you are not afraid to fail, you are more likely to take risks and try new approaches. This can lead to new solutions and ideas that would not have been discovered if you had been too afraid to take a chance. This can also lead to greater innovation and success in your personal and professional life.

Moreover, embracing failure helps to shift your focus from avoiding mistakes to learning from them. Rather than being afraid of failure, you become more focused on the process of learning and growth. This shift in mindset can help you to view failure in a positive light and see it as a natural part of the growth process.

Finally, it is important to remember that failure is not a personal attack, but rather a learning opportunity. When you embrace failure, you can let go of feelings of self-doubt and insecurity and focus on the benefits that come from learning and growth.

embracing failure is a critical component of the 10x revolution. By embracing failure, you can learn from your mistakes, build resilience and determination, increase creativity and innovation, shift your focus to learning, and let go of feelings of self-doubt. So, if you want to achieve great things and reach new levels of success, embrace failure and use it as an opportunity to learn and grow.

In order to understand the importance of this component, let's take a closer look at a few examples of how embracing failure can lead to success.

Example 1: In Starting a Business;

Starting a business can be a risky and challenging endeavor. There is a high likelihood of failure and many obstacles to overcome.

However, if you embrace failure as a natural part of the process, you will be better equipped to handle the challenges that arise and to persist in pursuing your goal.

For instance, let's say you start a business, but it fails. Instead of becoming discouraged and giving up, you embrace the failure and use it as a learning experience. You analyze the reasons for the failure and use that knowledge to make adjustments and improvements for your next attempt.

By embracing failure, you are better able to understand your weaknesses and strengths, and use this knowledge to create a more effective and successful business strategy. You also develop a more resilient and persistent mindset, which enables you to overcome the obstacles that might arise in the future.

Additionally, embracing failure can help you develop a more positive attitude towards risk-taking, which is a key ingredient for success in entrepreneurship. When you embrace failure, you become less afraid to take risks and more willing to pursue your goals, even in the face of uncertainty and challenges.

Example 2: In Pursuing a Career in Arts;

Pursuing a career in the arts can be a difficult and uncertain path. There is a high likelihood of rejection and many obstacles to overcome. However, if you embrace failure as a natural part of the process, you will be better equipped to handle the challenges that arise and to persist in pursuing your goal.

For example, let's say you pursue a career in the arts, but your work is rejected. Instead of becoming discouraged and giving up, you embrace the rejection and use it as a learning experience. You analyze the reasons for the rejection and use that knowledge to make adjustments and improvements for your next attempt.

By embracing failure, you are better able to understand the weaknesses and strengths of your work, and use this knowledge to create a more effective and successful artistic strategy. You also develop a more resilient and persistent mindset, which enables you to overcome the obstacles that might arise in the future.

Additionally, embracing failure can help you develop a more positive attitude towards taking creative risks, which is essential for success in the arts. When you embrace failure, you become less afraid to experiment and take creative risks, and more willing to pursue your artistic vision, even in the face of rejection and criticism.

Example 3: In Improving Athletic Performance;

Improving athletic performance can be a difficult and challenging endeavor. There is a high likelihood of failure and many obstacles to overcome. However, if you embrace failure as a natural part of the process, you will be better equipped to handle the challenges that arise and to persist in pursuing your goal.

For instance, let's say you set a goal to improve your athletic performance, but you fail. Instead of becoming discouraged and giving up, you embrace the failure and use it as a learning experience. You analyze the reasons for the failure and use that knowledge to make adjustments and improvements for your next attempt.

By embracing failure, you are better able to understand your limitations and strengths, and use this knowledge to create a more effective and successful athletic strategy. You also develop a more resilient and persistent mindset, which enables you to overcome the obstacles that might arise in the future.

Additionally, embracing failure can help you develop a more positive attitude towards risk-taking and pushing your limits, which is essential for success Mahatma Gandhi, a well-known leader in the Indian independence movement, is a prime example of embracing failure in order to achieve success. The 10x revolution, popularized by entrepreneur and author Grant Cardone, states that one should set goals 10 times larger than what they believe they can achieve in order to push themselves to their full potential. Gandhi embodies this principle through his relentless pursuit of independence and his unwavering determination in the face of failure.

Gandhi was born in 1869 in Porbandar, a coastal town in present-day Gujarat, India. Growing up, he was deeply influenced by the teachings of Hinduism and Jainism, which emphasized non-violence and truth-seeking. As a young man, Gandhi studied law in England and was admitted to the bar in 1891. After returning to India, he worked as a lawyer and became active in the Indian National Congress, a political organization dedicated to securing India's independence from British rule.

In 1915, Gandhi was sent to prison for the first time for leading a nonviolent protest against the British. Despite being arrested multiple times throughout his life, he continued to lead nonviolent protests and strikes, seeking to bring attention to the cause of Indian independence and to disrupt the British colonial government. Despite the success of these protests, the British government responded with violence, and Gandhi was often beaten and imprisoned.

However, Gandhi never let these failures defeat him. He believed that it was necessary to keep pushing forward, even in the face of setbacks and obstacles, in order to achieve his goal of independence for India. He embraced failure as a natural part of the journey, and saw it as an opportunity to learn and grow. He was known to say, "Strength does not come from physical capacity. It comes from an indomitable will."

Gandhi's determination and perseverance inspired millions of Indians to join the independence movement, and his leadership and non-violent approach helped to gain international attention and support for the cause. In 1947, India finally achieved independence from British rule, and Gandhi was celebrated as a hero of the nation.

Gandhi's life serves as a powerful example of the 10x revolution in action. He set his goal of independence for India at a level 10 times greater than what he believed was achievable, and he never let setbacks or failures discourage him from pursuing that goal. Through his relentless determination, he inspired millions of others to join the cause, and he eventually achieved the impossible.

Gandhi's embrace of failure as a natural part of the journey to success is a lesson that is just as relevant today as it was during his lifetime. In the fast-paced and competitive world we live in, it can be easy to get discouraged by setbacks and obstacles. However, just like Gandhi, we can choose to see failure as an opportunity to learn, grow, and achieve even greater success.

Mahatma Gandhi's life serves as a powerful testament to the 10x revolution and the power of embracing failure. He set his goal of independence for India at a level 10 times greater than what he believed was achievable, and he never let setbacks or failures discourage him from pursuing that goal. Through his relentless determination and unwavering spirit, he inspired millions of others to join the cause and eventually achieved the impossible. His legacy continues to inspire and motivate people all over the world to pursue their own goals with courage and determination, embracing failure as a natural part of the journey to success.

# CHAPTER SIX

## Knowledge is Power

Continuously seek knowledge and stay informed to increase your chances of success. The saying "knowledge is power" is a well-known phrase that has been around for centuries and is often attributed to philosopher Francis Bacon. In the context of the 10x revolution, this phrase takes on a deeper meaning and can be interpreted as having the power to transform your life and take you to the next level of success.

Knowledge, in this sense, is not just about having information or data stored in your brain. It is about actively seeking out new information and continually improving your understanding of the world. When you set a 10X goal, you are effectively setting a goal that requires you to learn new things, and in doing so, you are empowering yourself with the knowledge and skills necessary to achieve that goal.

For example, let's say you have a goal to earn $100,000 a year. While this may be a challenging goal, it may not be a 10X goal. A 10X goal in this case would be to earn $1 million a year. To achieve this goal, you would need to acquire new knowledge and develop new skills in areas such as sales, marketing, and financial management. By doing so, you would not only be working towards your goal, but you would also be empowering yourself with the knowledge and skills necessary to succeed in other areas of your life.

The power of knowledge can also be seen in the way it can impact your confidence and self-esteem. When you have a deeper understanding of a subject, you are more likely to feel confident in your abilities and more capable of facing challenges. This confidence can lead to greater success and a sense of achievement, which in turn can motivate you to continue learning and growing.

Furthermore, knowledge also has the power to provide you with a competitive edge. In today's fast-paced, globalized world, staying ahead of the curve and being knowledgeable in your field is more important than ever. By continuously learning and acquiring new knowledge, you are positioning yourself as a valuable asset in your workplace and setting yourself apart from others.

In conclusion, the saying "knowledge is power" is particularly relevant in the context of the 10x revolution. By setting large, 10X goals, you are forcing yourself to expand your knowledge and develop new skills, which in turn empowers you to achieve your goals and reach new levels of success. Furthermore, the acquisition of knowledge can lead to increased confidence, a competitive edge, and a sense of personal fulfillment. So, if you want to achieve great things and transform your life, remember that knowledge truly is power.

This component emphasizes the importance of acquiring knowledge and continuously learning and growing as a person.

Example 1: In Career Advancement;

In today's competitive job market, acquiring knowledge and continuously learning and growing is essential for career advancement. By staying informed about developments in your industry and acquiring new skills and knowledge, you can remain relevant and competitive, and increase your chances of success.

For example, let's say you work in a particular field, but you find that your knowledge is outdated. Instead of becoming discouraged, you embrace the opportunity to learn and grow. You seek out training and development opportunities, attend conferences, and read industry publications to expand your knowledge and skills.

By acquiring new knowledge and skills, you become more valuable to your employer, and increase your chances of being promoted or advancing in your career. Additionally, having a strong foundation of knowledge and skills can help you become a more effective leader, and better equipped to handle the challenges and opportunities that arise in your career.

Example 2: In Starting a Business;

When starting a business, knowledge is power. The more you know about your industry, your competition, and your target market, the better equipped you are to make informed decisions and take effective action.

For example, let's say you want to start a business in a particular field, but you lack knowledge about that industry. Instead of becoming discouraged, you embrace the opportunity to learn and grow. You research the industry, study your competition, and gain a deep understanding of your target market.

By acquiring knowledge about your industry, you are better equipped to make informed decisions, develop effective strategies, and compete in the marketplace. Additionally, having a deep understanding of your industry can help you identify opportunities and make the right connections, which can be critical for the success of your business.

Example 3: In Personal Growth;

Knowledge is also essential for personal growth. The more you know about yourself, your values, and your goals, the better equipped you are to make informed decisions and take effective action to achieve the life you desire.

For example, let's say you want to achieve a particular goal, but you lack knowledge or understanding about what it takes to achieve that goal. Instead of becoming discouraged, you embrace the opportunity to learn and grow. You research the goal, study successful people who have achieved that goal, and gain a deep understanding of what it takes to succeed.

By acquiring knowledge and understanding, you become better equipped to make informed decisions, develop effective strategies, and take action to achieve your goals. Additionally, having a deep understanding of yourself, your values, and your goals can help you live a more fulfilling life and become the person you want to be.

Whether you're pursuing a career, starting a business, or personal growth, having a strong foundation of knowledge and understanding can help you make informed decisions, develop effective strategies, and achieve your goals.

# CHAPTER SEVEN

## Time Management

Manage your time effectively and prioritize your activities to achieve your goals. The "Time Management" component of the 10x revolution emphasizes the importance of effectively managing your time to achieve your goals and maximize your potential. This component recognizes that time is a finite resource, and that how you choose to use your time can greatly impact your success and happiness.

Effective time management requires setting clear and achievable goals, prioritizing tasks based on their importance, and focusing your time and energy on the most important tasks. This means being mindful of how you spend your time, and making conscious decisions about how you want to allocate your time and energy.

"Time Management," is all about utilizing your time effectively and making the most of every moment. The 10x revolution suggests that by effectively managing your time, you can achieve 10 times the results in half the time, which is a powerful motivator for many people.

Effective time management is a key factor in success, as it allows you to prioritize your tasks, avoid distractions, and make the most of your time. By managing your time, you can increase your productivity, achieve your goals, and take control of your life.

Lets look at this scenario in Career Success

In today's fast-paced and competitive job market, it's essential to manage your time effectively in order to advance in your career. By focusing your time and energy on the most important tasks, you can increase your productivity, achieve your goals, and remain competitive.

For example, let's say you work in a particular field and you have a lot of responsibilities. Instead of becoming overwhelmed, you embrace the opportunity to manage your time effectively. You prioritize your tasks based on their importance, set specific and achievable goals, and focus your time and energy on the most important tasks. By effectively managing your time, you become more productive, achieve your goals, and increase your chances of success.

Lets look at this scenario in Starting a Business;

When starting a business, it's important to manage your time effectively in order to compete in the marketplace and achieve your goals. By focusing your time and energy on the most important tasks, you can increase your productivity, achieve your goals, and remain competitive.

For example, let's say you want to start a business in a particular field, but you have limited time and resources. Instead of becoming discouraged, you embrace the opportunity to manage your time effectively. You prioritize your tasks based on their importance, set specific and achievable goals, and focus your time and energy on the most important tasks. By effectively managing your time, you become more productive, achieve your goals, and increase your chances of success.

Lets look at this scenario in Personal Growth;

Time management is also essential for personal growth. By effectively managing your time, you can achieve your goals, pursue your passions, and enjoy a happy and fulfilling life.

For example, let's say you want to achieve a particular goal, but you feel like you don't have enough time. Instead of becoming discouraged, you embrace the opportunity to manage your time effectively. You prioritize your tasks based on their importance, set specific and achievable goals, and focus your time and energy on the most important tasks. By effectively managing your time, you become more productive, achieve your goals, and enjoy a happy and fulfilling life.

"Time Management" component of the 10x revolution emphasizes the importance of effectively managing your time to achieve your goals and maximize your potential. Whether you're pursuing a career, starting a business, or personal growth, managing your time effectively can help you become more productive, achieve your goals, and enjoy a happy and fulfilling life. By embracing the opportunity to manage your time effectively, and focusing your time and energy on the most important tasks, you can achieve success and become the best version of yourself.

Here are a few ways in which you can effectively manage your time and achieve success in accordance with the 10x revolution:

Make a To-Do List: Writing down your daily tasks and priorities is a great way to stay organized and focused. Make a list of all the tasks you need to complete, and prioritize them based on their level of importance.

Set Deadlines: Giving yourself a deadline for each task helps you focus and get things done. Make sure you are realistic about the amount of time it will take to complete each task and set a deadline accordingly.

Avoid Distractions: Distractions can be a major roadblock when it comes to getting things done. Avoid distractions by eliminating distractions, such as checking social media or email every few minutes. Instead, focus on the task at hand and give it your full attention.

Learn to Say No: Saying no to commitments that don't align with your goals is important in order to manage your time effectively. Don't take on tasks that are not a priority and focus on the tasks that will help you achieve your goals.

Use Technology to Your Advantage: Technology can be a great tool for managing your time. Utilize tools such as calendars, reminders, and productivity apps to help you stay on track.

Make Time for Self-Care: Taking care of yourself is just as important as completing your tasks. Make sure to set aside time for self-care activities, such as exercise, meditation, or hobbies, in order to maintain a healthy work-life balance.

Delegate Tasks: Delegating tasks to others can help you get more done in less time. Assign tasks to those who are capable and willing to complete them, and trust them to get the job done.

Limit Meetings: Meetings can take up a lot of time, so it is important to limit the number of meetings you attend. Make sure that any meetings you do attend are necessary and productive, and limit the amount of time you spend in meetings.

Take Breaks: Taking breaks is an important part of managing your time effectively. Taking regular breaks can help you stay focused, reduce stress, and increase productivity.

Evaluate and Adjust: Finally, it is important to evaluate and adjust your time management strategies on a regular basis. Look at what is working and what is not, and make changes as necessary to ensure that you are making the most of your time.

"Time Management," is a crucial aspect of success. By managing your time effectively, you can prioritize your tasks, avoid distractions, and make the most of your time. With effective time management, you can achieve your goals, increase your productivity, and take control of your life.

# CHAPTER EIGHT
## Eliminate Distractions

Eliminate distractions and focus on what is important. Emphasizes the importance of eliminating distractions in order to achieve success. Distractions can come in many forms, such as technology, social media, email, and other people, and can derail your focus and prevent you from reaching your goals. By eliminating distractions, you can increase your productivity, focus, and motivation, and ultimately achieve greater success.

One of the key benefits of eliminating distractions is increased focus. When you eliminate distractions, you can concentrate fully on the task at hand, which can lead to increased productivity and efficiency. This is because you are not constantly shifting your attention between different tasks and distractions, but rather focusing all of your energy on one thing.

In addition, eliminating distractions can also help to increase motivation. When you are not constantly being pulled away from your work, you are more likely to feel motivated and energized to keep moving forward. This can lead to a sense of momentum and progress, which can be incredibly motivating.

Moreover, eliminating distractions can also help to improve your mental and emotional wellbeing. Distractions can be incredibly stressful and can lead to feelings of anxiety and burnout. By eliminating distractions, you can reduce stress and improve your mental and emotional well-being, which can lead to greater happiness and success in all areas of your life.

Eliminating distractions also helps to prioritize your time and energy. By focusing on what is important and eliminating what is not, you can make the most of your time and energy, and achieve more in less time. This can be especially important for those with 10X goals, as you need to be able to maximize your resources in order to achieve your goals.

In addition, eliminating distractions can also help to improve relationships. When you are not constantly being pulled away from the people you care about, you can be more present and engaged, which can lead to stronger and more meaningful relationships.

It is important to remember that eliminating distractions is not a one-time process, but rather a ongoing effort. Distractions can be a constant challenge, but with the right tools and techniques, you can reduce the number and impact of distractions in your life. For example, you can turn off notifications on your phone, schedule focused work time, and practice mindfulness and meditation to reduce stress and increase focus.

By eliminating distractions, you can increase your focus, motivation, mental and emotional well-being, prioritize your time and energy, and improve your relationships. So, if you want to achieve great things and reach new levels of success, it is important to eliminate distractions and focus on what is important.

In this section, we will explore specific examples of how you can eliminate distractions and increase your success.

Turn off notifications on your phone: One of the biggest distractions in our lives is our phones. The constant stream of notifications, texts, calls, and emails can pull our attention away from what is important. To eliminate this distraction, turn off notifications on your phone during focused work times. This will help you stay focused on the task at hand and reduce stress and anxiety.

Schedule focused work time: Another way to eliminate distractions is to schedule focused work time. This means setting aside specific times during the day when you will only work on a specific task. During this time, turn off all distractions, such as notifications, and focus solely on the task at hand. This will help you stay focused and motivated, and increase your productivity and efficiency.

Practice mindfulness and meditation: Another way to eliminate distractions is to practice mindfulness and meditation. This can help to reduce stress and anxiety, and increase focus and motivation. By taking a few minutes each day to practice mindfulness or meditation, you can reduce distractions and increase your overall well-being.

Surround yourself with positive, motivated people: Another way to eliminate distractions is to surround yourself with positive, motivated people. This means surrounding yourself with people who will support and encourage you, rather than those who are negative or distract you from your goals. By doing this, you can reduce stress and anxiety, and increase your focus and motivation.

Use tools to increase focus and productivity: There are many tools available that can help you increase focus and productivity, such as time management apps, task management tools, and productivity software. By using these tools, you can eliminate distractions and increase your focus and efficiency, which can help you achieve great things.

Reduce social media usage: Social media can be a major distraction in our lives, and it is important to reduce or manage our usage of it. This can mean limiting your time on social media, or using tools to block or limit access to social media sites during focused work times. By doing this, you can reduce stress and anxiety, and increase your focus and productivity.

Avoid multitasking: Multitasking can be a major distraction, as it can reduce focus and productivity. Instead of trying to do multiple things at once, focus on one task at a time, and give it your full attention. This will help you stay focused, increase your productivity, and reduce stress and anxiety.

Create a distraction-free workspace: Another way to eliminate distractions is to create a distraction-free workspace. This means creating an environment where you can work without distractions, such as a quiet room or a designated workspace. By doing this, you can increase your focus and motivation, and reduce stress and anxiety.

There are many examples of how you can do it. By turning off notifications on your phone, scheduling focused work time, practicing mindfulness and meditation, surrounding yourself with positive, motivated people, using tools to increase focus and productivity, reducing social media usage, avoiding multitasking, and creating a distraction-free workspace, you can reduce distractions and increase your success. So, if you want to achieve great things and reach new levels of success, it is important to eliminate distractions and focus on what is important.

# CHAPTER NINE
## Surround Yourself with Success

This means surrounding yourself with individuals who have achieved success in their personal and professional lives, and who will support, motivate, and inspire you to reach new levels of success. By doing this, you can learn from others, gain new insights, and increase your motivation and focus. By surrounding yourself with successful individuals, you have the opportunity to learn from their experiences and knowledge, gain a better understanding of the mindset, habits, and behaviors necessary for success, and stay motivated by the examples they set. Furthermore, building relationships with successful individuals can also provide you with valuable connections and open doors to new opportunities that might not have been available otherwise.

However, simply being around successful individuals is not enough. You must actively engage with them, seek their guidance, and work to build strong relationships with them. This requires effort, but the benefits can be substantial and can help you accelerate your progress towards your own goals.

To further understand the impact of surrounding yourself with success, it's important to explore the concept of mindset. Your mindset is the set of beliefs and attitudes that you hold about yourself and the world around you. Your mindset has a profound impact on your thoughts, feelings, and actions, and ultimately, on the level of success you achieve. When you surround yourself with successful individuals, you have the opportunity to adopt their positive and growth-oriented mindset, which can help you think and act at a higher level. This can help you overcome limiting beliefs and negative self-talk that may have been holding you back and keep you motivated to reach your goals.

In addition, surrounding yourself with successful individuals can also help you develop new skills and acquire new knowledge. When you are around people who are successful, they are likely to share their experiences, insights, and expertise with you. This can help you expand your skill set and knowledge base, which can be invaluable as you work to achieve your own goals. Furthermore, by learning from their experiences, you can avoid making the same mistakes they did and instead, leverage their success to reach your desired outcomes faster.

The power of networks and relationships should also be noted when discussing the impact of surrounding yourself with success. The people you surround yourself with can play a significant role in the opportunities that come your way and the level of success you ultimately achieve. By building relationships with successful individuals, you can access their networks and gain introductions to individuals who can help you advance your goals. Furthermore, by working with successful individuals, you can demonstrate your skills, knowledge, and determination, which can help you build your own network and reputation.

It's also important to consider the impact of surrounding yourself with success on your motivation and drive. When you surround yourself with individuals who have already achieved what you want to achieve, you are exposed to what is possible. This exposure can help you stay motivated and inspired as you work towards your own goals, as you can see that success is achievable. Furthermore, when you see others achieving their goals and reaching new heights of success, you are likely to feel a sense of urgency and a desire to keep up, which can drive you to take even more massive and determined action.

Another important aspect to consider when surrounding yourself with success is the idea of accountability. When you surround yourself with successful individuals, they are likely to hold you accountable to your goals and to your commitment to success. This can help you stay focused and on track, and ensure that you are taking the necessary steps to reach your desired outcomes. Furthermore, by holding yourself accountable to others, you are more likely to follow through on your plans and stick to your commitments, which can be critical to achieving success.

It's also worth mentioning that surrounding yourself with success doesn't mean you need to surround yourself with individuals who are exactly like you. In fact, diversity can bring a wealth of new perspectives, experiences, and knowledge to the table. By surrounding yourself with individuals who have a diverse set of skills, knowledge, and experiences, you can gain new insights, learn new approaches to problem-solving, and expand your own skill set and knowledge base. Furthermore, diversity can also challenge you to think outside the box and consider new and innovative solutions to your problems, which can be invaluable as you work to achieve your goals.

In conclusion, the idea of "surrounding yourself with success" is a critical component of the 10x revolution, and involves surrounding yourself with individuals who can inspire, motivate, and help you achieve your goals. By doing so, you can learn from their experiences, gain valuable insights, and make valuable connections that can help you reach new heights of success. You can adopt a growth-oriented mindset, expand your skill set and knowledge base, and stay motivated and driven as you work towards your desired outcomes. By surrounding yourself with success, you can take your life and career to the next level and achieve the success you have always wanted. Here are few ways on how to surround yourself with success:

Seek out mentorship: One way to surround yourself with success is by seeking out mentorship. This means finding someone who has achieved success in your field or in an area you are interested in, and who is willing to guide and support you. A mentor can provide you with valuable insights, advice, and support, and help you navigate the challenges and obstacles you may face on your journey to success.

Join professional organizations: Another way to surround yourself with success is by joining professional organizations. These organizations provide opportunities to network with like-minded individuals, attend events and conferences, and gain access to resources and training that can help you achieve success. By participating in these organizations, you can expand your knowledge, make valuable connections, and gain new perspectives.

Attend conferences and events: Attending conferences and events is another way to surround yourself with success. By attending these events, you can meet other successful individuals, hear from experts and thought leaders, and learn about the latest developments in your field. Additionally, attending these events can provide you with opportunities to network and make valuable connections that can help you achieve success.

Seek out successful individuals for guidance and support: Another way to surround yourself with success is by seeking out successful individuals for guidance and support. This means finding individuals who have achieved success in your field or in an area you are interested in, and who are willing to offer guidance and support. By doing this, you can gain valuable insights, advice, and support that can help you reach new levels of success.

Join a mastermind group: Joining a mastermind group is another way to surround yourself with success. A mastermind group is a group of individuals who come together to share ideas, provide support and guidance, and help each other reach new levels of success. By participating in a mastermind group, you can learn from others, receive valuable feedback, and gain new perspectives that can help you achieve success.

Surround yourself with positive and motivated individuals: Surrounding yourself with positive and motivated individuals is another key aspect of surrounding yourself with success. This means surrounding yourself with individuals who are positive, motivated, and supportive, rather than those who are negative or unsupportive. By doing this, you can increase your motivation and focus, reduce stress and anxiety, and increase your chances of success.

Seek out opportunities to collaborate and work with others: Another way to surround yourself with success is by seeking out opportunities to collaborate and work with others. This means working with others to achieve a common goal, such as a project or business venture. By collaborating with others, you can gain new insights, expand your knowledge, and increase your chances of success.

Read books, blogs, and articles from successful individuals: Another way to surround yourself with success is by reading books, blogs, and articles from successful individuals. This means reading about the experiences and insights of individuals who have achieved success, and learning from their successes and failures. By doing this, you can gain new perspectives, expand your knowledge, and increase your chances of success.

There are many examples of how you can do it. By seeking out mentorship, joining professional organizations, attending conferences and events, seeking out successful individuals for guidance and support, joining a mastermind group, surrounding yourself

# CHAPTER TEN

## Never Stop Growing

This means continuously seeking out new knowledge, skills, and experiences, and constantly working to improve yourself and reach new levels of success. The idea is that success is not a destination, but a journey that requires continuous learning and growth. One of the key reasons why it's important to never stop growing is that personal and professional growth is essential for success. In today's fast-paced and rapidly changing world, new technologies, industries, and opportunities are emerging all the time. To be successful, it's essential that you continuously learn and adapt to these changes and stay ahead of the curve. Furthermore, personal and professional growth can also help you stay motivated and engaged, as you are always working towards new goals and milestones.

The concept of continuous growth is also closely tied to the idea of a growth mindset. A growth mindset is the belief that you can grow and develop through effort and learning. When you have a growth mindset, you view challenges and failures not as setbacks, but as opportunities for growth and learning. This mindset can help you stay motivated and focused on your goals, even when faced with obstacles or setbacks.

Another reason why it's important to never stop growing is that growth can help you stay relevant and competitive. In today's job market, it's critical to stay ahead of the curve and be able to offer valuable skills and knowledge. By continuously developing yourself, you can stay ahead of the competition and remain relevant in your field. Furthermore, growth can also help you expand your skill set and knowledge base, which can make you more valuable to your organization and increase your earning potential.

The idea of never stopping growing also extends to personal development. Personal growth can help you become a more well-rounded, confident, and happy individual. This can have a positive impact on all areas of your life, including your relationships, your health, and your overall sense of well-being. By continually working on personal growth, you can become a better version of yourself and live a more fulfilling life.

One of the key ways to never stop growing is to continually set new goals. When you set new goals, you create a sense of purpose and direction, and you are always working towards something new and exciting. This can help you stay motivated and focused, and can also help you continually measure your progress and see the results of your efforts. Furthermore, by setting new goals, you can continuously stretch yourself and challenge yourself to grow and develop in new ways.

Another way to never stop growing is to continually seek out new learning opportunities. This can include taking courses, attending workshops and conferences, reading books, and engaging in other forms of professional and personal development. By continuously seeking out new learning opportunities, you can stay ahead of the curve, expand your skill set and knowledge base, and keep yourself motivated and engaged.

It's also important to cultivate a strong support system and surround yourself with individuals who will support and encourage your growth. By having supportive individuals in your life, you have a network of people who can help you stay motivated, offer advice and guidance, and cheer you on as you work towards your goals. Furthermore, by surrounding yourself with individuals who are also committed to growth and development, you can learn from each other, support each other, and hold each other accountable to your goals.

In conclusion, the idea of "never stopping growing" is a critical component of the 10x revolution, and involves continuously developing and improving yourself, both professionally and personally. By doing so, you can stay relevant and competitive, become a better version of yourself, and live a more fulfilling life. Here are some ways on how to never stop growing: Invest in personal development: One way to never stop growing is by investing in personal development. This means taking courses, attending workshops, reading books, and engaging in other activities that help you expand your knowledge, skills, and abilities. Personal development can help you grow both personally and professionally, and can provide you with the tools and resources you need to reach new levels of success.

Seek out new experiences: Another way to never stop growing is by seeking out new experiences. This means trying new things, taking risks, and stepping outside your comfort zone. By doing this, you can gain new insights, learn from your failures, and develop new skills and abilities that can help you achieve success.

Set goals: Setting goals is another way to never stop growing. By setting goals, you can focus your efforts, measure your progress, and stay motivated and on track. Setting both short-term and long-term goals can help you stay focused and driven, and can provide you with a roadmap for success.

Surround yourself with individuals who are always learning:

Surrounding yourself with individuals who are always learning is another way to never stop growing. This means seeking out individuals who are constantly seeking out new knowledge, skills, and experiences, and who are motivated and driven to improve themselves. By doing this, you can learn from others, gain new insights, and be inspired to reach new levels of success.

Stay curious and ask questions: Staying curious and asking questions is another key aspect of never stopping growing. This means being open to new ideas, perspectives, and experiences, and constantly seeking to expand your knowledge and understanding of the world. By doing this, you can gain new insights, develop new skills, and reach new levels of success.

Take time to reflect: Taking time to reflect is another way to never stop growing. This means taking time to reflect on your experiences, both good and bad, and to learn from them. By doing this, you can gain new insights, identify areas for improvement, and develop new strategies for success.

Stay open-minded: Staying open-minded is another key aspect of never stopping growing. This means being open to new ideas, perspectives, and experiences, and avoiding being rigid or closed-minded. By staying open-minded, you can gain new insights, expand your knowledge, and reach new levels of success.

Embrace change: Embracing change is another way to never stop growing. This means being open to new ideas, opportunities, and experiences, and being willing to adapt and change in response to new challenges and opportunities. By embracing change, you can grow and evolve, and reach new levels of success.

Never stop growing is an important component of the 10x

revolution, and there are many examples of how you can do it. By investing in personal development, seeking out new experiences, setting goals, surrounding yourself with individuals who are always learning, staying curious and asking questions, taking time to reflect, staying open-minded, and embracing change, you can continuously improve yourself and reach new levels of success. The likes of Elon Musk, Mark Zuckerbeg, Jeff Bezos, Larry Page, Bill Gates, Richard Branson and lots more has adapt the 10x revolution to reach new levels of success.

www.ingramcontent.com/pod-product-compliance
Lightning Source LLC
Chambersburg PA
CBHW071143220526
45467CB00015B/1810